Ana Cláudia Rodovalho ▪ Karina Torres F. Silva ▪ Luciana Renda B. Melo

Spaghetti Kids

EDIÇÃO ATUALIZADA

5º ANO

Student's Book

MACMILLAN

Table of Contents

Unit		Pages
1	Let's review!	4
	Extra work	12
2	He's jumping!	14
	Extra work	22
3	It's hot today!	24
	Extra work	32
4	My clothes	34
	Extra work	42
1-4	Review	44
5	My father is a doctor	46
	Extra work	54
6	Making friends!	56
	Extra work	64
7	What time is it?	66
	Extra work	74
8	My daily routine	76
	Extra work	84
5-8	Review	86
	Word List	88
	Special Projects	91
	Stickers	

INTRODUCTION

CHARACTER PRESENTATION

Unit 1 • Lesson 1

LET'S REVIEW!

1. Classify the words. Write the corresponding number.

2	fifteen
	fridge
	basketball
	eleven
	chair

3	stove
	soccer
	fifty
	swimming
	bathroom

1	kitchen
	twenty
	bedroom
	bed
	dining room

4	tennis
	closet
	volleyball
	three
	living room

2. Unscramble the words and complete the pictures.

1.

KONYEM

____

2.

RAZBE

____

3.

TELAHNPE

____

4.

NSEAK

____

5.

REITG

____

6.

OINL

____

Unit 1 • Lesson 2

1. Look at the code and write the numbers.

60

____

70

____

80

____

90

____

100

____

A B C D E F G H I J K L M

N O P Q R S T U V W X Y Z

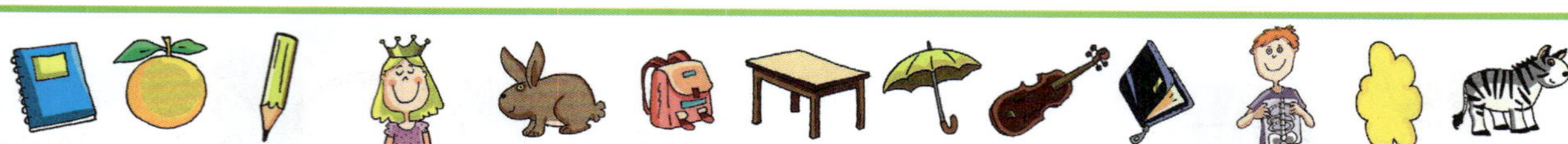

2. Solve the problems and write the numbers.

1. 42 + 35 = *77 seventy-seven*
2. 100 – 35 = ______________
3. 65 + 23 = ______________
4. 87 – 20 = ______________
5. 88 + 3 = ______________
6. 56 + 44 = ______________

3. Memory game

Unit 1 • Lesson 3

1. Read the sentences and draw a line.

She can play soccer.
They can't swim.
He can't play tennis.
He can cook.
They can jump.
She can run.

2. LET'S SING!

IF YOU ARE HAPPY

If you're happy and you know it,
clap your hands.
If you're happy and you know it,
clap your hands.
If you're happy and you know it,
then your face will surely show it.
If you're happy and you know it,
clap your hands.

3. Learn about your friend. complete

NAME	CAN	CAN'T
Kenji	*He can dance.*	

Unit 1 • Lesson 4

1. Find the words and write them in the correct column.

F	J	A	N	U	A	R	Y	T	T	M	A	R	C	H	N
E	E	E	R	A	P	S	D	U	B	E	P	E	F	W	O
B	E	R	H	R	I	A	F	E	T	E	R	O	R	E	V
R	T	A	L	S	L	T	S	S	W	W	I	W	I	D	E
U	K	D	J	R	M	U	K	D	J	U	L	Y	D	N	M
A	U	G	U	S	T	R	A	A	L	A	R	A	A	E	B
R	L	S	N	V	M	D	N	Y	W	O	Y	T	Y	S	E
Y	M	U	E	B	A	A	O	C	T	O	B	E	R	D	R
M	O	N	D	A	Y	Y	S	E	Y	I	S	C	O	A	W
I	H	D	A	D	N	N	T	H	U	R	S	D	A	Y	E
P	H	A	C	D	W	O	A	D	E	C	E	M	B	E	R
U	Y	Y	E	Q	S	S	E	P	T	E	M	B	E	R	E

DAYS OF THE WEEK	MONTHS OF THE YEAR	
	January	

2. Listen and check.

1. 

2. 

3. 

4. 

5. 

3. What's the month? Write the names.

BRAZILIAN CALENDAR

January

February

______

April

May

______

______

______

______

October

______

December

EXTRA WORK

Unit 1

1. Circle the odd one out.

Farm animals	cow	zebra	pig	horse
Toys	bicycle	puzzle	snake	teddy bear
Parts of the house	table	living room	kitchen	bathroom
Days of the week	Sunday	Monday	Thursday	basketball
Sports	soccer	balloon	basketball	tennis
Activities	run	jump	pig	swim
Holidays	Christmas	Easter	teacher	Carnival

2. Count and write.

How many…?

1.  *One teacher* in my classroom.

2.  ____________________ in my house.

3. 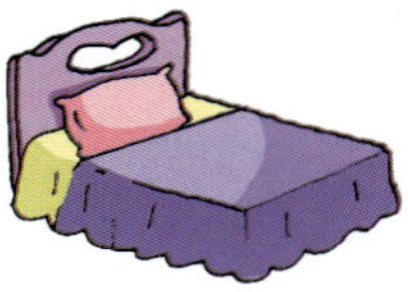 ____________________ in my house.

4.  ____________________ in my classroom.

5.  ____________________ in my classroom.

6.  ____________________ in my classroom.

7.  ____________________ in my classroom.

8. 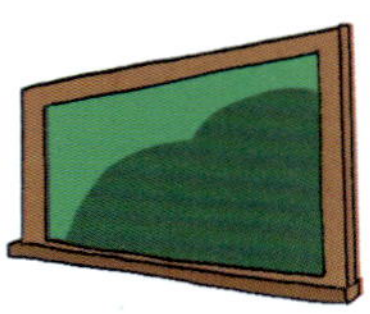 ____________________ in my classroom.

Unit 2 • Lesson 5

HE'S JUMPING!

1. Write the words under the pictures.

Run	Play soccer	Swim
Jump	Skate	Ride a bike

2. Unscramble and stick.

NCEAD

dance

KTESA

____

MUPJ

____

WTCHA TV

____

IWMS

____

LPAY CERCSO

____

3. Listen to the sound and circle.

1.	jump	skate	run
2.	swim	play soccer	ride a bike
3.	watch TV	jump	play soccer
4.	skate	ride a bike	jump
5.	dance	swim	play soccer
6.	swim	watch TV	ride a bike

Unit 2 • Lesson 6

VALUES
KEEP FIT

1. Listen and read.

It is a beautiful day. The children are in the park. Ann is running. Paulo is jumping. Kenji is playing soccer. Luciana is swimming. Suzana is skating and Francisco is riding a bicycle. They are happy!

2. Match

( ) He is running. — 1

( ) He is skating. — 2

( ) He is swimming. — 3

( ) He is playing soccer. — 4

( ) He is dancing. — 5

3. Yes (Y) or No (N)? Listen and write.

1  (   )

2  (   )

3  (   )

4  (   )

5  (   )

6  (   )

4. Draw and talk.

Unit 2 • Lesson 7

1. What's wrong?

Read and circle the problems in the picture.

The children are on the beach. Suzana is jumping. Ann is running. Francisco is playing soccer and Kenji is swimming. Luciana is running. Paulo is dancing. They are having fun!

2. Let's have fun!

3. Game

Unit 2 • Lesson 8

1. Unscramble the sentences.

1. IS / SOCCER / PLAYING / HE ______________________
2. SHE / DANCING / IS ______________________
3. SWIMMING / SHE / IS ______________________
4. BIKE / A / HE / RIDING / IS ______________________
5. HE / JUMPING / IS ______________________
6. TV / THEY / WATCHING / ARE ______________________

2. Now match the sentences in exercise 1 to the pictures.

( ) 

(1) 

( ) 

( ) 

( ) 

( ) 

PROJECT

Cut pictures from magazines.

Glue the pictures.

Write sentences.

Tell your friends.

EXTRA WORK

Unit 2

1. Wordsearch

O V B N N W Q A Z # I C O O K
G O # T O # T H E # B E A C H
P L A Y # B A S K E T B A L L
L W E R C X C V U I L K H G B
S P R U N M B # L M J U M P G
W E R T F F G N M J I L # I D
I A S B N M K I L P X Z C V Y
M N H # M K I W A T C H # T V

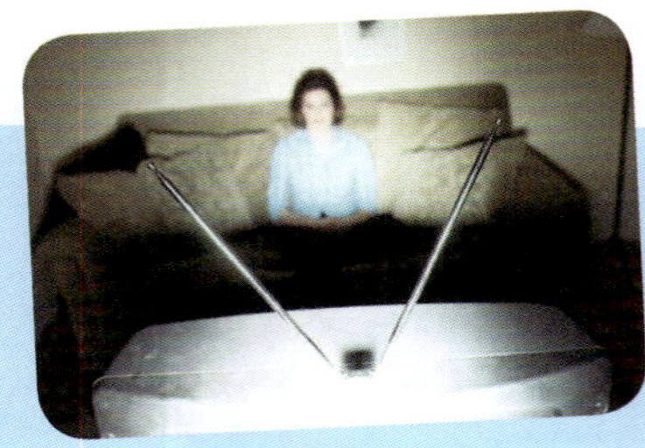

2. Read and label the pictures.

a. We are at the park. We are skating.

b. We are at home. We are dancing.

c. We are at school. We are playing soccer.

d. We are on the beach. We are swimming.

e. We are at the park. We are playing volleyball.

Unit 3 • Lesson 9

IT'S HOT TODAY!

1. Listen and read.

2. Stick

hot

rainy

cold

sunny

windy

snowy

cloudy

3. Crossword

4 5 6

W E A T H E R

3

2 7

1

1

2

3

5

4

6

7

Unit 3 • Lesson 10

1. Look at the pictures and write sentences.

fly a kite

watch TV

ride a bike

play video games

make a snowman

1. It's sunny.

   I can ______________________________________

   I can't ______________________________________

2. It's windy.

   I can ______________________________________

   I can't ______________________________________

3. It's rainy.

   I can ______________________________________

   I can't ______________________________________

4. It's snowy.

   I can ______________________________________

   I can't ______________________________________

2. Find the words and complete the sentences.

S	D	F	T	C	C	F	M
S	C	S	G	L	M	L	U
S	C	U	D	O	O	Y	K
W	S	N	G	U	M	T	U
I	D	N	N	D	W	Y	T
M	G	Y	D	Y	I	W	G
U	D	R	O	C	I	K	O
P	S	N	O	W	M	A	N
R	W	T	Y	U	I	O	M
P	L	A	Y	C	O	V	B
G	T	M	T	U	C	E	T
D	R	T	V	F	R	O	T

It's ____________ I can go to the beach.

It's rainy. I can't ____________ at the park.

It's snowy. I can make a ____________

It's windy. I can ____________ my kite.

It's ____________ I can't go to the park.

It's hot. I can ____________

3. LET'S SING!

IT'S RAINING!

It's raining (× 3) and wet today.
Let's stay in (× 3) and play.

It's snowing (× 3) and cold today.
Let's make a snowman, make a snowman today.

It's cloudy (× 3) and windy today.
Let's stay in (× 3) and play.

It's sunny (× 2),
It's hot and sunny today.
Let's go out (× 3) and play.

Hooray!

Unit 3 • Lesson 11

1. Complete with the words from the box.

hot – sunny – cold – snowy – windy

IN THE USA: fall

IN ENGLAND: autumn

THE FOUR SEASONS

SPRING

It's s u n n y.

WINTER

It's ___ ___ ___ ___

and ___ ___ ___ ___ ___ .

FALL

It's ___ ___ ___ ___ ___

and rainy.

SUMMER

It's ___ ___ ___

and sunny.

2. Listen and circle.

1.	summer	winter	fall
2.	spring	fall	summer
3.	summer	spring	winter
4.	spring	fall	summer

3. Read.

Now talk to your friends and write the answers.

FRIEND	WHAT'S YOUR FAVORITE SEASON?	WHAT CAN YOU DO?

Unit 3 • Lesson 12

1. Read and complete the chart.

MY FAVORITE SEASON IS . IT IS  AND . I CAN ,  AND . I CAN'T .

FAVORITE SEASON	
WEATHER	
CAN	
CAN'T	

2. What's your favorite season? Draw a picture and complete the sentences.

My favorite season is ____________________

It's ____________________

I can ____________________

I can't ____________________

PROJECT

Make a weather chart.

THE WEATHER

EXTRA WORK

Unit 3

1. Read and match.

1. It's cold and rainy.
   Let's watch TV.

2. It's hot and sunny.
   Let's go out and play.

a

b

c

d

e

2. Now, write about the other pictures.

b. *It's windy. Let's...*

3. Cut and glue pictures from magazines.
Use the words from the box to write about your region.

snowy
cloudy
sunny
rainy
cold
hot
windy

SPRING	SUMMER
It's...	It's...

FALL	WINTER

Unit 4 • Lesson 13

MY CLOTHES

1. Write the words next to the pictures according to the colors.

jacket shorts dress sweater

boots sneakers jeans T-shirt

2. Listen and check the answers.

3. Put the sentences in the correct places.

WHAT'S THE WEATHER LIKE? **WHAT COLOR ARE YOUR SOCKS?**
MY RED T-SHIRT AND MY WHITE SKIRT. **IS IT A T-SHIRT?**

Unit 4 • Lesson 14

1. Wordsearch

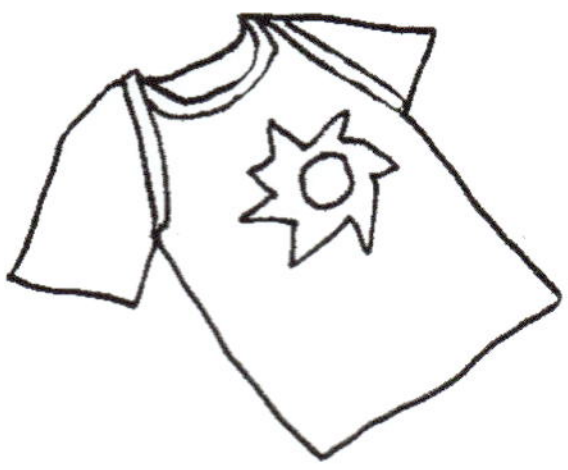
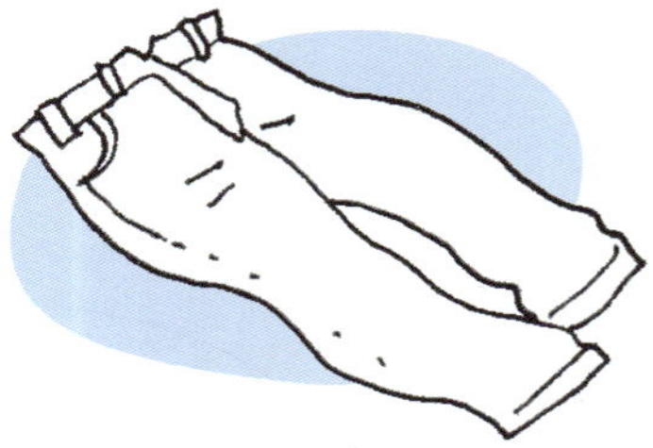

Q	J	O	V	D	R	E	S	S	D	S	O	B
A	A	W	W	P	P	S	W	X	R	H	O	O
E	C	T	-	S	H	I	R	T	T	O	T	O
N	K	U	S	I	L	I	Q	N	-	R	-	T
J	E	A	N	S	J	E	M	N	P	T	D	S
S	T	-	Z	L	O	E	C	W	S	S	F	H
U	O	O	M	N	S	N	E	A	K	E	R	S

2. Read the sentences and color the pictures in exercise one.

- The dress is yellow.
- The jacket is black.
- The T-shirt is green.
- The boots are brown.
- The shorts are white.
- The jeans are blue.
- The sneakers are red.

3. Answer

What are your favorite clothes?

Draw here your favorite clothes:

What color are they?

What color is your school uniform?

What can you wear in the winter?

4. Now talk to your friends. Use the questions in exercise 3.

Unit 4 • Lesson 15

1. Listen and circle.

1. 

2. 

3. 

4. 

5. 

6. 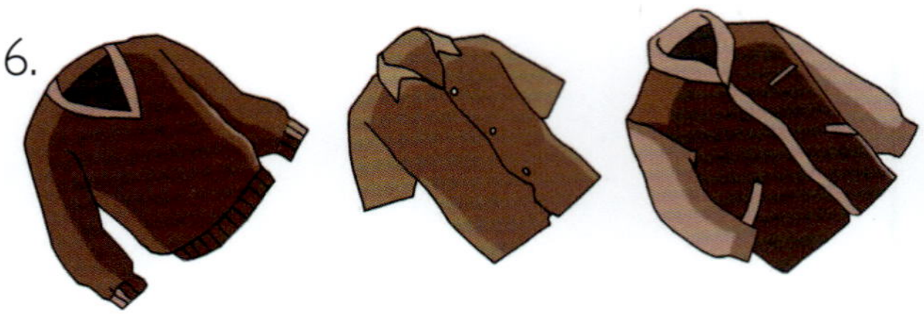

2. LET'S SING!

MY CLOTHES

s-w-e-a-t-e-r, d-r-e-s-s (x2)
These are my clothes,
my clothes, my clothes.
g-l-o-v-e-s, b-o-o-t-s (x2)
These are my clothes,
my clothes, my clothes.

s-h-o-r-t-s, j-e-a-n-s (x2)
These are my clothes,
my clothes, my clothes.
Now it's your time.
Spell and rhyme.

3. Stick and complete the window.

Unit 4 • Lesson 16

1. Read and answer the questions.

1. What color is the jacket?

____

2. How many T-shirts are there?

____

3. What color are they?

____

4. Is the dress yellow?

____

5. What color are the boots?

____

2. Pay attention to your friends' clothes and complete the chart.

Number of friends with...	
Sneakers	
Jacket	
Hat	
Sweater	
Skirt	
White socks	
Glasses	

3. Play hangman with your friend. Use these words:

SWEATER – SOCKS – JACKET – SNEAKERS – SKIRT – T-SHIRT BOOTS – DRESS – SHORTS – JEANS – GLASSES

Unit 4

1. Cut the pictures and glue them on the correct picture.

He's wearing ______________________________

She's wearing ______________________________

2. Look at the picture and complete the story.
Use the words in the box.

MY BEDROOM IS A MESS. MY JEANS ARE UNDER THE _________ . MY _______________ ARE IN THE CLOSET. MY SCHOOLBAG IS _________ THE CHAIR. MY BOOTS ARE _________ THE CHAIR. MY DRESS IS _________ THE BED AND MY PHOTOS ARE _________ THE _________ .

on		sneakers
in	on	closet
bed		under

Units 1-4 • Review

1. Look at the pictures and choose the correct sentence.

1.		He's jumping.	He's playing soccer.	He's swimming.
2.		She's jumping.	She's running.	She's skating.
3.		He's riding a bike.	He's playing soccer.	He's skating.
4.		She's riding a bike.	She's skating.	She's playing soccer.

2. Circle the odd one out.

1. sweater	shorts	playing	boots
2. swimming	playing	winter	running
3. hot	red	cold	snowy
4. dress	spring	summer	fall
5. blue	yellow	windy	black

3. Crossword

Unit 5 • Lesson 17

MY FATHER IS A DOCTOR

1. Listen and read.

2. Unscramble these words according to the colors.

T D D N S P F E O E U T O I A C N R U L R C T T S D I

E H O I E E C F E R S N E I R T T O G F H F T I E C R E R

T *eacher* ______________

D ______________

D ______________

N ______________

S ______________

P ______________

F ______________

3. Listen and stick.

1. Secretary
2. Doctor
3. Pilot
4. Driver
5. Lawyer
6. Engineer
7. Architect

Unit 5 • Lesson 18

1. Put the words under the right pictures.

~~TEACHER~~ – PILOT – DRIVER – DENTIST – NURSE
DOCTOR – POLICE OFFICER – FIREFIGHTER

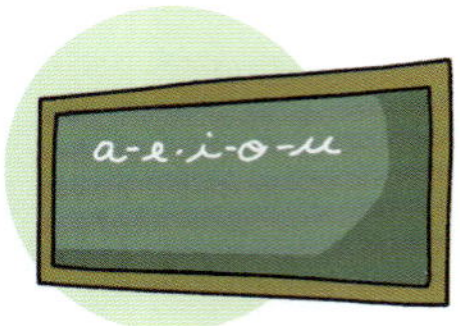

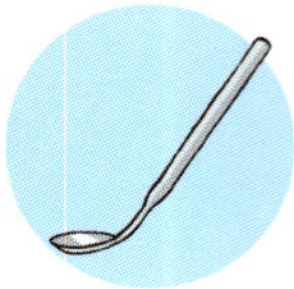

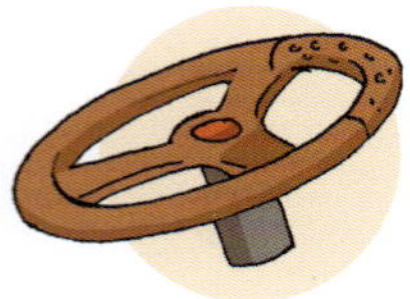

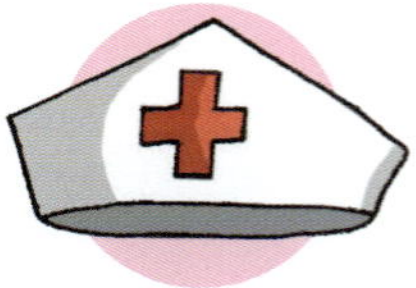

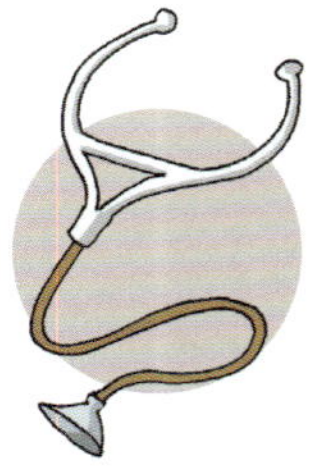

2. Help Mário go to work.

3. Match and complete the sentences.

VALUES
VALUE ALL JOBS

Maria

Ted

Miguel

Caroline

Harumi

Carlos

firefighter

dentist

police officer

doctor

teacher

nurse

1. Maria is a ______________________
2. Ted is a ______________________
3. Caroline is a ______________________
4. Miguel is a ______________________
5. Harumi is a ______________________
6. Carlos is a ______________________

Unit 5 • Lesson 19

1. Read Ben's blog.

Now, answer the questions:

What's the girl's name? ________________________

Is Tricia a teacher? ________________________

Is Michael a student? ________________________

Is Tom a dentist? ________________________

2. Complete the sentences.

My father is a ____________ and my mother is a ____________

I am a ________________________

3. What do you want to be when you grow up?

____

4. Listen and cross out the incorrect picture.

1.

2.

3.

4.

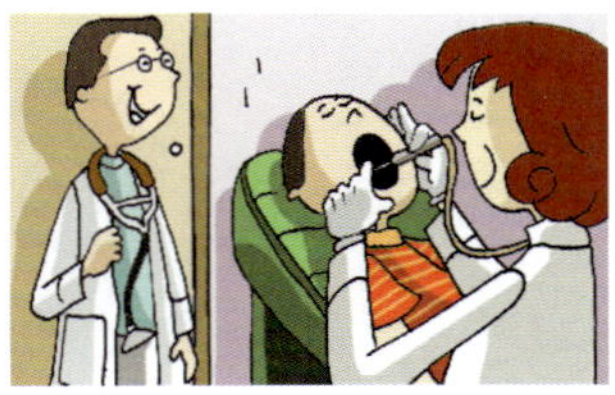

5.

6.

Unit 5 • Lesson 20

1. LET´S SING!

WORK, WORK, WORK ALL DAY

(verse 1)
Well, I'm a **doctor.**
I work all day.
I'm at the **hospital**
Every day.
(chorus)
Work, work, work, work
Work, work, work, work
I work all day!
(verse 2) Pilot / airport
(verse 3) Firefighter / fire station

2. Game

PROJECT

Draw your family tree.

Write sentences.

Tell your friends.

EXTRA WORK

Unit 5

1. Cut and glue the pictures on the correct name tags.

HOSPITAL
Alison Cant
DOCTOR

HEALTH CARE
Kevin Bowser
Dentist

AIR FORCE
Ken Star
PILOT

HOSPITAL
Jennifer White
NURSE

construction
Wendy May
ENGINEER

TRANS
Paul Redman
DRIVER

2. Wordsearch. Find the names of the jobs.

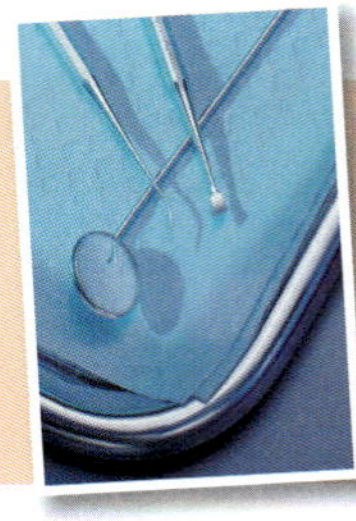

W	N	U	R	S	E	P	Y	D	E	N	T	I	S	T
S	T	G	Y	V	Y	E	T	B	J	B	G	N	N	G
C	Y	P	T	F	T	N	E	G	R	P	E	H	F	E
D	T	O	E	#	E	G	W	#	E	I	W	T	E	W
O	E	L	W	E	W	I	S	W	C	L	X	V	V	X
C	W	I	S	W	S	N	X	X	Z	O	F	R	X	F
T	S	C	X	T	X	E	W	F	A	T	R	I	#	R
O	X	E	W	E	W	E	F	R	Q	U	S	D	O	S
R	W	#	F	A	F	R	C	#	E	J	R	E	P	R
E	F	O	C	C	C	T	X	R	P	H	I	R	K	I
D	C	F	X	H	X	R	W	I	I	F	O	I	L	O
C	X	F	W	E	W	A	R	C	H	I	T	E	C	T
V	W	I	R	R	R	E	W	I	C	E	T	T	T	P
N	V	C	Q	A	E	Z	#	R	V	R	I	Y	Y	O
Y	F	E	R	A	X	C	V	Q	X	F	P	Q	E	I
H	R	R	R	F	I	R	E	F	I	G	H	T	E	R

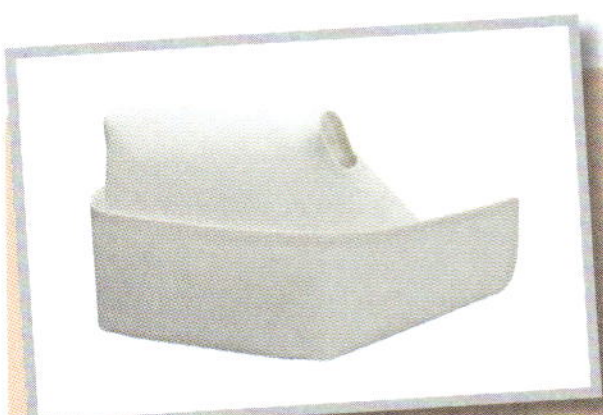

Unit 6 • Lesson 21

MAKING FRIENDS!

1. Listen and read.

2. Read

3. Look at the pictures and circle the correct word.

1 

His / Her name is Ann.

2 

His / Her name is Kenji.

3 

His / Her name is Paulo.

4 

His / Her name is Suzana.

Unit 6 • Lesson 22

1. Listen and read.

2. Match

1. She is tall and thin. She is pretty.
2. He's old and short.
3. He's thin and tall. He's young.
4. It's red and ugly.
5. She's fat.
6. He's short and fat.

3. Write sentences about your family. Use these words.

PRETTY	OLD	TALL	FAT	THIN	SHORT	YOUNG

Unit 6 • Lesson 23

1. *Yes or No?*

	YES	NO
1. She's ugly.		
2. She's thin.		
3. Her hair is black.		
4. She's young.		
5. She's short.		

2. Listen and check.

1

2

3

4

5

6

3. Read the text and answer the questions.

Look at this photo. These are my grandparents: Alberto and Ana. They are very old!

My grandfather is tall and thin. He's really nice. I love his stories.

My grandmother isn't tall. She's short. She has green eyes and gray hair. I love her food!

Is Alberto young? ______________________________

Is Ana tall? ______________________________

Is Alberto thin? ______________________________

Is Ana old? ______________________________

4. Draw a famous person and write three sentences about him/her.

____

____

____

____

____

Unit 6 • Lesson 24

1. Complete the chart about yourself and glue your photo.

Name: ____________________

Age: ____________________

Pet: ____________________

Favorite food: ____________________

Favorite color: ____________________

Favorite number: ____________________

Can: ____________________

Can't: ____________________

Have: ____________________

2. Complete the text about a friend.

complete

______ name is ______ . ______ is ______ years old.

______ pet is a/an ______ . ______ favorite food is ______ .

______ favorite color is ______ . ______ mother is a/an

______ and ______ father is a/an ______ .

______ can ______ and ______ .

______ can't ______ or ______ .

______ is ______ and ______ .

______ eyes are ______ and ______ hair is ______ .

3. LET'S SING!

TALL OR SHORT

Tall or short
Young or old
Fat or thin
That's you and me (x2)

Sometimes good and
Sometimes bad
Sometimes happy and
Sometimes sad

That's you and me
You and me

EXTRA WORK

Unit 6

1. Look at the pictures and write what is different.

IN PICTURE A:

There is a big present.

There is...

IN PICTURE B:

There is a small present.

There is...

2. Look at the pictures and circle the correct word.

1. Caio is tall / short.
2. Ivan is fat / thin.
3. Caio's hair is brown / black.
4. Ivan's eyes are blue / brown.
5. Ivan's hair is brown / black.
6. Caio's eyes are blue / brown.

Unit 7 • Lesson 25

WHAT TIME IS IT?

1. Listen and read.

2. Stick the words under the correct picture.

LOOK!

Noon = 12 o'clock in the middle of the day

AM (= from midnight until noon)

Midnight = 12 o'clock at night

PM (= from noon until midnight)

3. Read.

4. Answer the questions.

1. What time is your favorite TV program? My favorite TV program is at ________
2. What time is your English class? My English class is at ________
3. What time do you have lunch? I have lunch at ________
4. What time do you go to bed? I go to bed at ________

1. Look and talk.

2. Complete

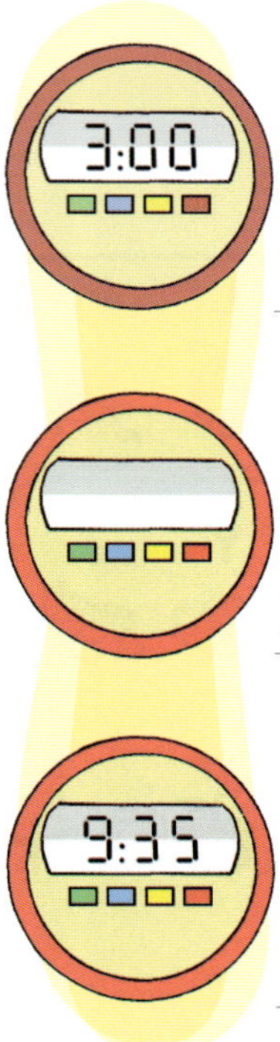

______________________ It's eleven thirty.

____

____

It's ten fifteen. ______________________

______________________ It's seven o'clock.

____

3. What time is it? Check the correct column.

		YES	NO
1.	It's eleven o'clock.		
2.	It's seven forty-five.		
3.	It's six twenty.		
4.	It's eight o'clock.		
5.	It's two twenty.		
6.	It's six twenty-five.		
7.	It's eleven ten.		
8.	It's twelve o'clock.		

Unit 7 • Lesson 27

1. Look at the code and write the actions.

1  

______________ ______________________________

2  

______________ ________________

3  

______________ ____________________

4  

______ ________________________

5  

______ ______ __________________

6  

______ ________________________

2. Match

1.  6:30 a.m.

2.  6:45 a.m.

3.  7:00 a.m.

4.  12:20 p.m.

5.  4:00 p.m.

6.  7:30 p.m.

3. Complete

1. I do my homework at ______________________________

2. I have breakfast at ______________________________

3. I go to school at ______________________________

4. I get up at ______________________________

5. I have lunch at ______________________________

Unit 7 • Lesson 28

VALUES
BE PUNCTUAL

1. Listen and draw the hands of the clocks.

1.

2.
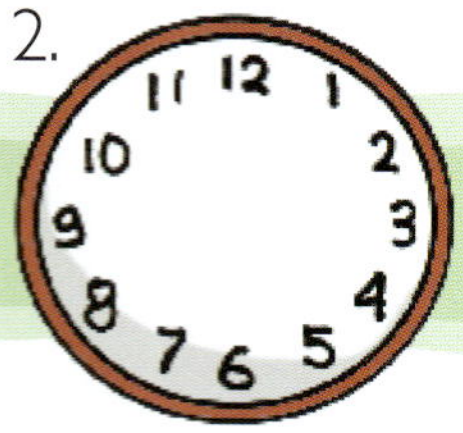

3.

4.

5.

6.

2. Write the words under the appropriate column.

LUNCH	WATCH TV	GET UP
TWO THIRTY	SEVEN FORTY-FIVE	DO HOMEWORK
DINNER	TEN TWENTY	BREAKFAST

ACTIONS	TIME	MEALS

3. Game

12:10	2:00	4:00
8:10	3:00	1:15
10:20	7:35	7:35

10:35	5:40	8:15
1:25	:00	4:45
3:00	2:50	7:00

5:00	6:30	7:05
2:50	10:55	1:20
11:00	4:40	5:40

EXTRA WORK

Unit 7

1. What time is it? Complete the chart about you and your friend.

1. go to bed
2. go to school
3. eat
4. swim
5. play soccer
6. watch TV

	YOU	YOUR FRIEND
1. go to bed		
2. go to school		
3. eat		
4. swim		
5. play soccer		
6. watch TV		

2. Write the time.

3. Complete the information about Mike. complete

7:30

12:00

3:20

5:40

8:15

9:55

1	7:30	*It's time to go to school.*
2	12:00	________________
3	3:20	________________
4	5:40	________________
5	8:15	________________
6	9:55	________________

MY DAILY ROUTINE

1. Number the pictures.

2. Listen and check your answers.

3. Crossword

2

1

3

4

5

6

Unit 8 • Lesson 30

1. Unscramble the words and stick.

1	TGE PU	
2	KAET A HWERSO	
3	HURBS YM TTEEH	
4	STILEN OT SUMIC	
5	THWAC VT	
6	VHAE HUNCL	
7	OG OT EBD	
8	OD MEOWRKHO	

2. Listen and read.

3. Answer about you.

1. What time do you get up?

____

2. What time do you go to bed?

____

3. What time do you take a shower?

____

4. Now talk to your friend using the questions in exercise 3. Complete the chart.

NAME			

Unit 8 • Lesson 31

1. Look at the pictures and complete the text.

MY NAME IS PAULA. I ______________ AT SIX FORTY-FIVE.
I ______________ AND ______________
I ______________ AT SEVEN THIRTY. I ______________
AT TWELVE O'CLOCK. I ______________ WITH MY FAMILY.
I ______________ AT FOUR O'CLOCK. AT SIX
TWENTY-FIVE I ______________
I ______________ AND ______________

2. Now complete Paula's diary.

3. Listen and choose the right answer.

1. ☐ I get up at 6:30.
   ☐ I have breakfast at 6:30.

2. ☐ I take a shower at 7 o'clock.
   ☐ I go to school at 7 o'clock.

3. ☐ I have lunch at 12 o'clock.
   ☐ I go home at 12 o'clock.

4. ☐ I play soccer at 3:30.
   ☐ I take a shower at 3:30.

5. ☐ I do my homework at 4 o'clock.
   ☐ I watch TV at 4 o'clock.

6. ☐ I have dinner at 6:45.
   ☐ I do my homework at 6:45.

7. ☐ I watch TV at 8 o'clock.
   ☐ I listen to music at 8 o'clock.

8. ☐ I listen to music at 9:30.
   ☐ I go to bed at 9:30.

Unit 8 • Lesson 32

1. Game

PROJECT

Cut pictures from magazines.

Glue the pictures.

Write the time.

Write sentences.

Tell your friends.

Unit 8

1. Write your daily activities in the correct places.

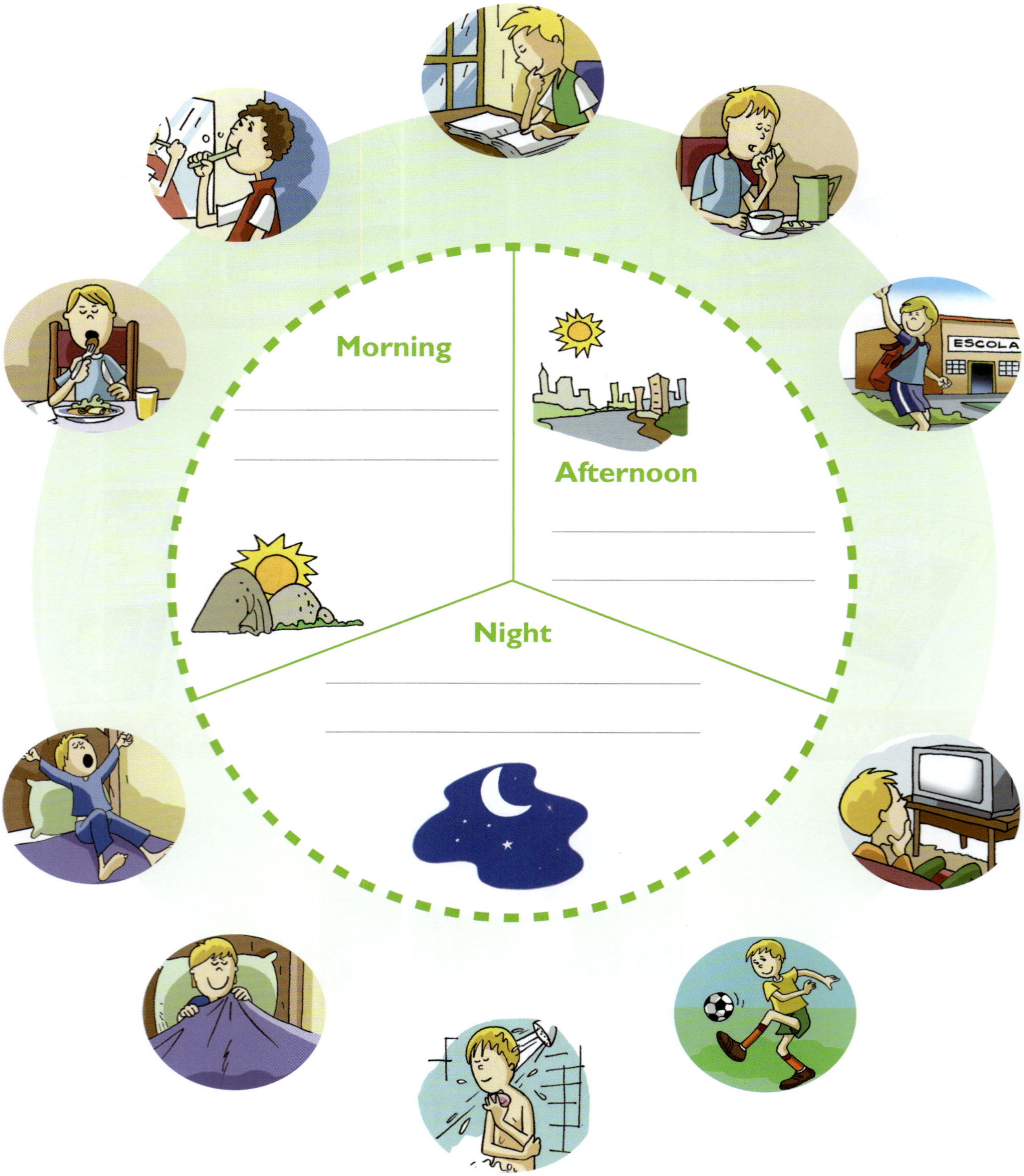

2. Break the code and read the letter.

Now we're at the end of Spaghetti Kids 5° ano.

I know a lot of new things.

I can speak about my ____ ,

my ____, my ____ and

my daily ____, in English.

I know many new words. I can count from ____ to ____

____ and I can ____.

Oh, and I can sing cool ____ !

Learning English is very ____ ! What about you? What can you do in English?

Units 5-8 • Review

1. Choose a word. Draw it.
Can your friend say what it is?

DOCTOR
POLICE OFFICER
TEACHER NURSE
FIREFIGHTER
STUDENT ENGINEER
SECRETARY

2. Write the professions in the man, the daily routines in the square, the times in the clock and the adjectives in the girl.

SIX O'CLOCK
GET UP
YOUNG
TEACHER
THIN
DOCTOR
GO TO SCHOOL
SEVEN FORTY-FIVE
TEN TWENTY
HAVE LUNCH
FIREFIGHTER
POLICE OFFICER
PRETTY
BRUSH MY TEETH
ELEVEN THIRTY
DENTIST

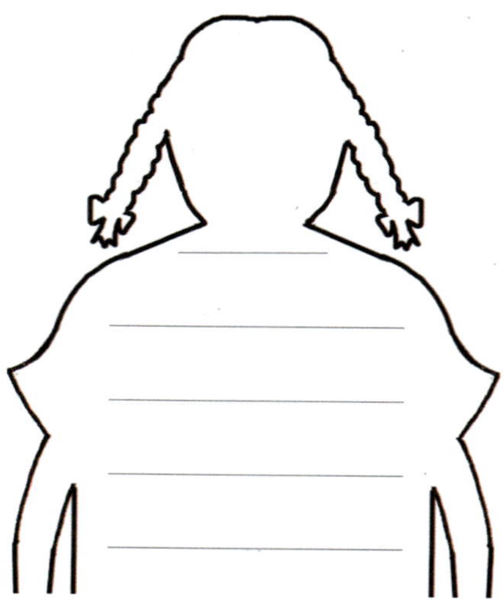

3. Game

START HERE

What time is it?

What time do you play soccer?

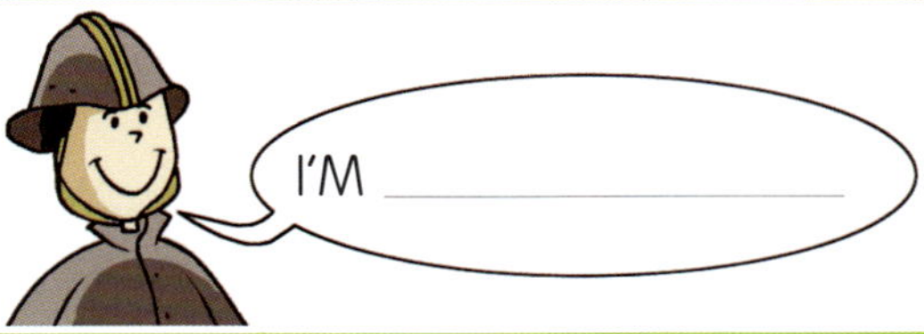

She's ______

What time do you have lunch?

What time is it?

What color is it?

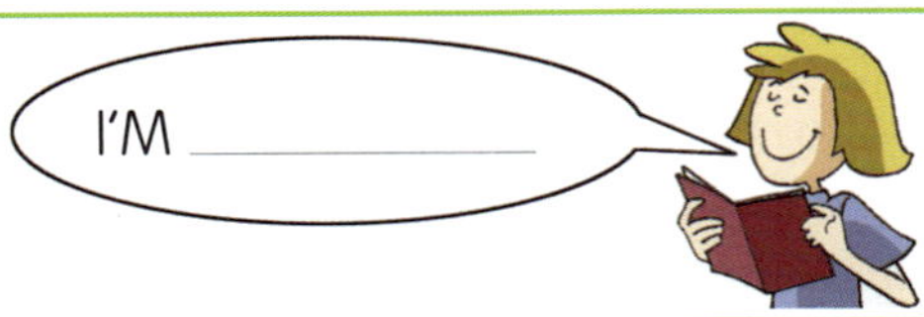

What time do you listen to music?

He's ______

Congratulations!
You're the winner.

START HERE

What time is it?

What time do you take a shower?

He's ______

What time do you have dinner?

What time is it?

What color is it?

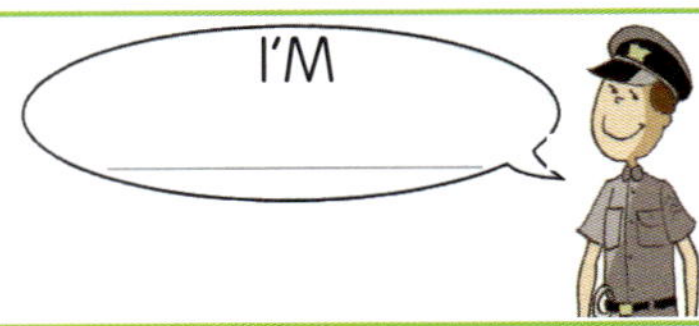

What time do you go home?

She's ______

Congratulations!
You're the winner.

Word List

A

according to – de acordo com
action – ação
age – idade
airport – aeroporto
answer – responder
April – abril
architect – arquiteto(a)
August – agosto
aunt – tia
autumn – outono (inglês britânico)

B

bad – ruim, má
ball – bola
basketball – basquete
bathroom – banheiro
beach – praia
beautiful – bonito(a)
bed – cama
bedtime – hora de dormir
bedroom – quarto
bike – bicicleta
black – preto(a)
blue – azul
boots – botas
breakfast – café da manhã
brown – marrom
brush my teeth – escovar meus dentes

C

can – poder
chair – cadeira
chart – tabela
children – crianças
clap your hands – bater palmas
class – aula
closet – armário embutido
clothes – roupas
cloudy – nublado
code – código
cold – frio
color – cor
cook – cozinhar
correct – correto(a)
cousin – primo(a)
cross out – assinalar
crossword – palavra cruzada
cut – cortar, recortar

D

daily – diário(a)
dance – dançar
day – dia
December – dezembro
dentist – dentista
dining room – sala de jantar
dinner – jantar
do – fazer
doctor – médico(a)
dress – vestido
driver – motorista

E

eat – comer
elephant – elefante
engineer – engenheiro(a)
exercise – exercício
eyes – olhos

F

face – rosto
fall – outono (inglês americano)
family – família
family tree – árvore genealógica
famous – famoso(a)
fat – gordo(a)
father – pai
favorite – favorito(a)
February – fevereiro
firefighter – bombeiro(a)
fly a kite – soltar pipa
food – comida
Friday – sexta-feira
fridge – geladeira
friend – amigo(a)
furniture – móvel

G

game – jogo
get up – levantar
glasses – óculos
glue – colar
go – ir
go home – ir para casa
go out – sair
good – bom, boa
good night – boa noite
grandfather – avô
grandmother – avó
gray – cinza
green – verde
grow up – crescer
guess – adivinhar

H

hair – cabelo
hands of the clock – ponteiros do relógio
happy – feliz, contente
Happy birthday – feliz aniversário
hat – chapéu, boné
have – ter
have dinner – jantar
have fun – divertir-se
have lunch – almoçar
help – ajudar
her – dela
here – aqui
his – dele
homework – lição de casa
hot – quente

I

I don't know – eu não sei
incorrect – incorreto(a)

J

jacket – jaqueta
January – janeiro
July – julho
jump – pular
June – junho

K

kitchen – cozinha
know – saber

L

lawyer – advogado(a)
lion – leão
listen – ouvir
living room – sala de estar
lunch – almoço

M

magazines – revistas
make – fazer
March – março
May – maio
meals – refeições
meet – conhecer
midnight – meia-noite
Monday – segunda-feira
monkey – macaco
month – mês
mother – mãe
music – música

N

name – nome
noon – meio-dia
November – novembro
number – número
nurse – enfermeiro(a)

O

October – outubro
old – velho(a)

P

park – parque
parts – partes
person – pessoa
pet – animal de estimação
photo – foto
picture – figura
pilot – piloto
pink – cor-de-rosa
play – jogar
police officer – policial

pretty – bonita
problems – problemas
project – projeto

Q

questions – perguntas

R

rainy – chuvoso
read – ler
red – vermelho(a)
review – revisar
ride a bike – andar de bicicleta
routine – rotina
run – correr

S

sad – triste
Saturday – sábado
school – escola
seasons – estações
secretary – secretária
sentences – sentenças
September – setembro
short – baixo(a)
show – mostrar
sing – cantar
snake – cobra
sneakers – tênis
snowman – boneco de neve
snowy – com neve
soccer – futebol
socks – meias
sometimes – algumas vezes
spider – aranha
sports – esportes
spring – primavera
squares – quadrados
stay in – ficar em casa
stove – fogão
student – aluno(a)
summer – verão
Sunday – domingo
sunny – ensolarado
sweater – suéter
swim – nadar
swimming – natação

T

take a shower – tomar banho (de chuveiro)
tall – alto(a)
teacher – professor(a)
tell – contar
tennis – tênis
text – texto
thin – magro(a)
Thursday – quinta-feira
tiger – tigre
time – hora
go to bed – ir domir, ir para a cama
today – hoje
too – também
T-shirt – camiseta
Tuesday – terça-feira
TV program – programa de TV

U

ugly – feio
uncle – tio
under – embaixo
uniform – uniforme

V

volleyball – vôlei

W

want – querer
watch TV – assistir à TV
wear – usar, vestir
weather – tempo
Wednesday – quarta-feira
week – semana
wet – úmido
what – o que, qual
when – quando
white – branco(a)
windy – com ventos
winter – inverno
work – trabalhar
write – escrever
wrong – errado

Y

year – ano
yellow – amarelo(a)
young – jovem
your – seu, sua, seus, suas
yourself – você mesmo(a)

Spaghetti Kids

EDIÇÃO ATUALIZADA

Special Projects

A Clock

YOU NEED:

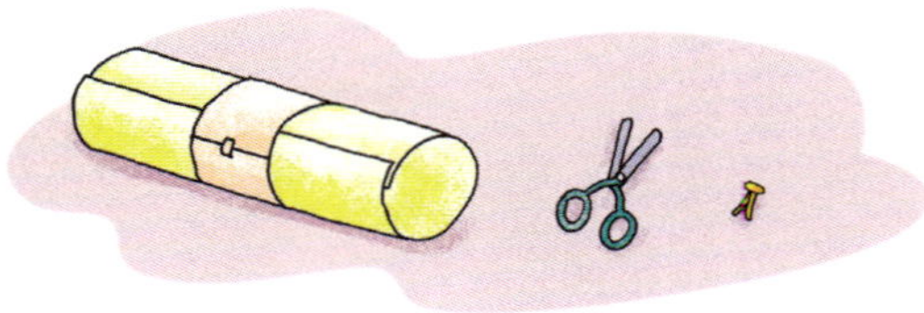

STEPS:

1

2

3

4

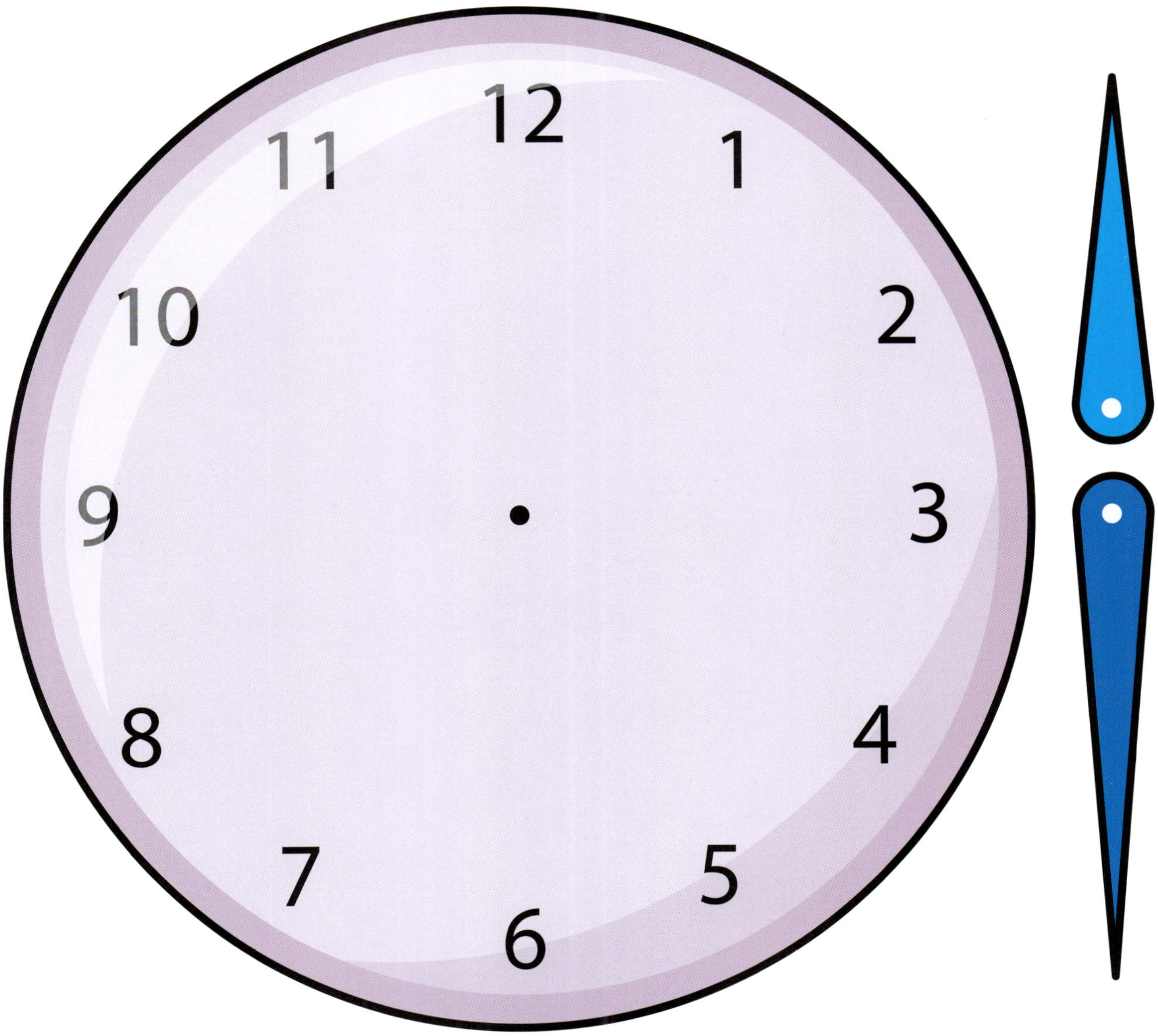

Dominoes

YOU NEED:

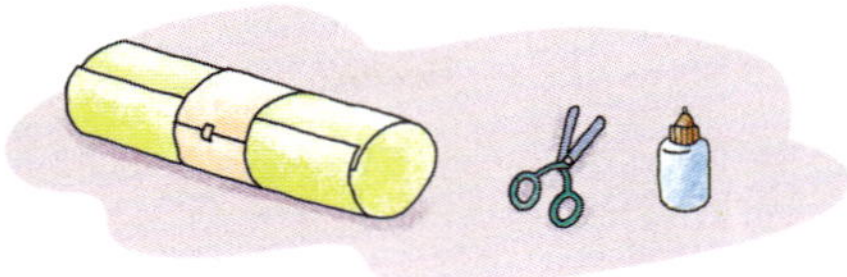

STEPS:

teacher – police officer
firefighter – police officer
teacher – doctor
nurse – nurse
doctor – nurse
doctor – doctor

teacher – teacher
firefighter – nurse
police officer – dentist
firefighter – firefighter
dentist – doctor
dentist – firefighter

dentist – teacher
dentist – dentist
dentist – nurse
police officer – doctor
police officer – police officer
firefighter – teacher

nurse – police officer
doctor – teacher
firefighter – dentist
teacher – nurse
police officer – nurse
firefighter – doctor

A Town

YOU NEED:

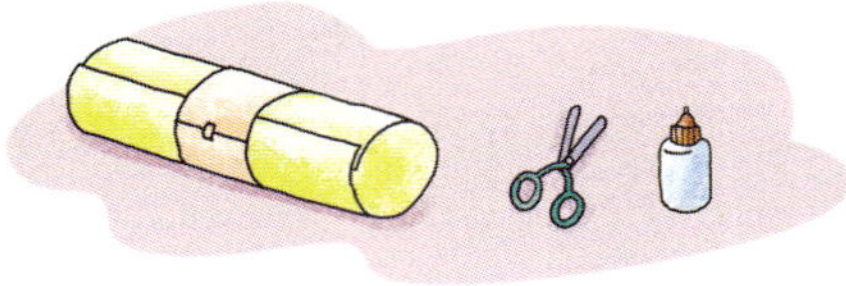

STEPS:

1

2

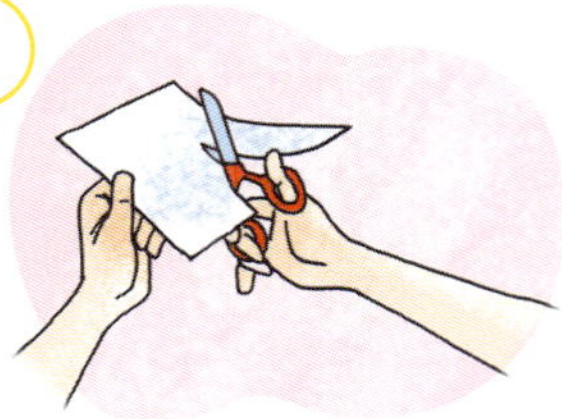

3

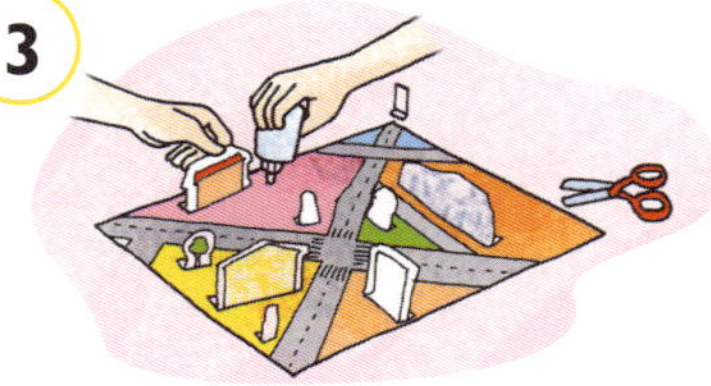

DICA

Recorte também as figuras das páginas 99 e 101 para formar uma maquete. Use-a para criar uma história. Você e seus colegas podem juntar suas maquetes e formar uma cidade.

A Town

A Town

A diary

Complete your diary with your daily routine.

Now, decorate your diary.

MACMILLAN

Editora: Wilma Moura
Editora assistente: Ana Paula Landi
Assistente editorial: Glauce Perusso Pereira Dias Muniz

Edição de arte, projeto gráfico, capa, editoração eletrônica: AMj Studio
Ilustrações: Gaiola Estúdio, Paulo Borges (Projects) e Amilton Ishikawa/AMj Studio

Fotos: © 2008 Jupiterimages Corporation

Dados Internacionais de Catalogação na Publicação (CIP)
(Câmara Brasileira do Livro, SP, Brasil)

Rodovalho, Ana Cláudia
Spaghetti kids : 5° ano / Ana Cláudia Rodovalho, Karina Torres F. Silva, Luciana Renda B. Melo. -- 4. ed. atual. -- São Paulo : Macmillan, 2008.

ISBN 978-85-74186-47-4 (student's book)
ISBN 978-85-74186-42-9 (teacher's book)

1 . Inglês (Ensino fundamental) I. Silva, Karina Torres F. II. Melo, Luciana Renda B. III. Título.

08-02383 CDD-372.652

Índices para catálogo sistemático:
1. Inglês : Ensino fundamental 372.652

4ª edição - 2008
Macmillan do Brasil
Rua José Felix de Oliveira, 383 – Granja Viana – 06708-645 – Cotia – São Paulo – Brasil
Atendimento ao professor: São Paulo – Capital – (0XX11) 4613 2278
Demais localidades: 0800 168877 – Fax: (0XX11) 4612 6098
E-mail: elt@macmillan.com.br - Website: www.macmillan.com.br

impresso no Brasil -Ricargraf - nov/2018

STICKERS

ÁG. 15

ÁG. 25

STICKERS

ÁG. 39

ÁG. 47

STICKERS

PÁG. 55

BREAKFAST

LUNCH

DINNER

PÁG. 64